HAYNES EXPLAINS
AMERICANS

Owners' Workshop Manual

© Haynes Publishing • Written by **Boris Starling**

Published in October 2017

A catalogue record for this book is available from the British Library

ISBN 978 1 78521 151 5

Haynes Publishing, Sparkford, Yeovil,
Somerset BA22 7JJ, UK
Tel: +44 (0) 1963 440635
Website: www.haynes.com

Haynes North America, Inc.,
861 Lawrence Drive, Newbury Park,
California 91320, USA

Printed and bound in Malaysia

Cover image from Getty Images

Illustrations taken from the
Haynes Rover 820, 825 & 827
Owners Workshop Manual

Written by **Boris Starling**
Edited by **Louise McIntyre**
Designed by **Richard Parsons**

THE
MANUAL

Safety first!

There are two main reasons why safety is paramount when it comes to the US.

1) The country is full of guns.
2) The country is full of lawyers.

Sometimes points 1 and 2 overlap, which means you have a lawyer with a semi-automatic in one hand and a subpoena in the other. Either way, safety first is best practice if you want to avoid (a) being shot (b) being sued (c) shooting the person who sued you (d) suing the person who shot you.

Working facilities

Working facilities vary considerably according to your exact location within the United States of America. In New York City, you may well find yourself 75 floors up in a strange environment known as a 'trading floor' surrounded by people barking 'sell 400 UTX at 120'. In Wyoming, you are more likely to be the only human being within 1,000 square miles, though with plenty of buffalo, bison, bears and moose for company. In Florida, take your pick of alligators and pensioners: in other words, of wrinkly-skinned bathers or alligators.

Contents

Introduction

A Texan rancher was visiting a farm in Scotland. The Scottish farmer showed his visitor round the farm.

'This is the farmhouse where I live with my wife and bairns,' said the Scotsman.

The Texan was unimpressed. 'I got a doghouse back home that's bigger than that.'

'And this is my tractor,' said the Scotsman, indicating his new Massey Ferguson.

'That tiny little thing? You serious? We got kids' toys that are bigger than that.'

Determined to play the good host, the Scotsman pressed on. 'These here are my cattle. Magnificent, aren't they?'

'How many you got?'

'Oh, 500 or so.'

The Texan snorted in derision. 'Five hundred? Five hundred?! I got 50,000 of the darn beasts, I tell you.'

The tour went on in this way until they were back at the farmhouse.

'That it?' said the Texan when they'd finished.

'That's it. 300 acres of Scotland's finest.'

'300 acres is what we in Texas call a backyard. Lemme tell you something. Back home I get in my car before the sun comes up, and I drive and drive and drive all day, and by the time the sun goes down I'm only halfway across my land.'

'Oh aye,' the Scotsman replied. 'I used to have a car like that once.'

About this manual

The aim of this manual is to help you get the best value from the Americans. It can do this in several ways. It can help you (a) decide what work must be done (b) tackle this work yourself, though if you are a large corporation, you may choose to have much of it performed by external contractors such as a call centre in Malaysia or a small army of illegal immigrant workers.

Although the specific requirements of the American can vary slightly according to age, socio-economic status and region, fundamentally they all want variations on the following: somewhere serving a quadruple-layer burger with at least a dozen different ingredients, a gun range with sufficient firepower on site to end a small war and start a bigger one, 478 TV channels and a car the size of the Queen Mary – you know, just as a runaround.

⚠ Dimensions, weights and capacities

Overall height

Men .... 5'9". And no, we're not converting that into centimetres for you. Work it out for yourself.

Women .... 5'3". 6'3" when wearing power heels for Silicon Valley board meetings.

Willis Tower .... 1,451'. Bruce Willis 5'11". WhatchootalkinboutWillis? 4'8".

Overall weight

Average man .... 195lb. Hoping to break the 200lb barrier by 2020.

Average woman .... 168lb. Has permanent option of shifting unsightly lard by getting rid of husband.

Consumption

Burgers and fries ...... 14 times a week. (Having them for breakfast as well as lunch and dinner would just be rude.)

Beer .... with an alcohol content of 2%, roughly 144fl oz is enough to (a) give you a very mild buzz (b) have you peeing like Niagara Falls for the next 24 hours.

Engine

Stroke .... more likely if eating habits are anything to go by.

Power.......................... to be fought (Public Enemy), of love (Jennifer Rush), to the people (John Lennon).

Torque .... radio shock jocks, late night chat shows, filibustering politicians.

Bore .... the small Oregon town of Boring (pop: 8,000. Last time anything interesting happened there: 1973.) Twinned with Dull in Scotland.

Redline .... at any attempt by the Federal Gumment to come and take our guns away, yes sir.

Interior

It's now almost 250 years since America fought for and won independence from the British, yet in many ways the Americans still see themselves as those freedom fighters of yesteryear. They may have every conceivable gadget, pill and modern convenience to make life as comfortable as possible, but in their heads they are frontiersmen and pioneers. They see themselves as individuals always on their guard against an overreaching federal government.

This is why the Second Amendment to the Constitution (for a nation so obsessed with winning, this is pretty much the only time that the word 'second' is acceptable) is so iconic in America. The Second Amendment gives the right to bear arms (as opposed to the right to bare arms, which is less controversial, but you should still put sunblock on even if it's a cloudy day), and this in turn is why you can find high-powered automatic weapons next to the fishing rods in outdoor stores.

Americans genuinely believe they live in the best country in the

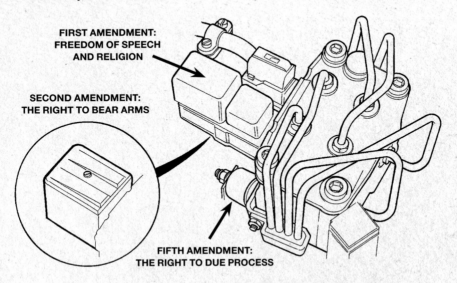

FIRST AMENDMENT:
FREEDOM OF SPEECH
AND RELIGION

SECOND AMENDMENT:
THE RIGHT TO BEAR ARMS

FIFTH AMENDMENT:
THE RIGHT TO DUE PROCESS

FIG 10•1 **THE WAY IT ALL CONNECTS – THE AMERICAN MINDSET**

world. For the many millions who don't have passports, it may as well be the only country in the world (they think of Canada and Mexico as extensions of Minnesota and California respectively). A foreign tourist in America will be asked several times a day 'how do you like it here?' and woe betide anyone who says anything vaguely negative.

For now at least, America is the world's leading superpower, and their people are justifiably proud of that and of the traditions of democracy, freedom and egalitarianism which have come with it. Not for nothing did Superman equate 'truth and justice' with 'the American way'. Nowadays, of course, Superman would spend five hours in the airport immigration queue patiently explaining why Krypton (a) hadn't issued him a passport (b) didn't appear between Kiribati and Kuwait on the list of UN countries.

Americans see themselves as hardworking: to say of someone that they 'get things done' is a high compliment. They like action, and if they're not doing something then they would at least like people to think they're doing something. They also see themselves as patriotic. For many countries, flags are flown mainly at official buildings or on national holidays. In the USA, they are flown anywhere anytime.

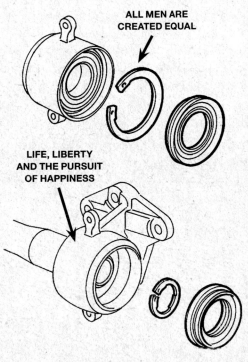

ALL MEN ARE CREATED EQUAL

LIFE, LIBERTY AND THE PURSUIT OF HAPPINESS

FIG 10•2 **FITTING IT ALL TOGETHER: THE DECLARATION OF INDEPENDENCE**

Famous Americans born on 4 July include tennis player Pam Shriver, President Calvin Coolidge and army veteran turned activist Ron Kovic (who was played by Tom Cruise in *Born On The Fourth Of July*).

Exterior

How the Americans see the British

For many Americans, *Downton Abbey* was not so much a drama as a documentary. These same Americans (a) believe that British people still sit around in bowler hats having tea and cucumber sandwiches at exactly 4pm (b) are even more ardent royalists than those amiable lunatics in Union Jack suits who camp outside hospital for a week just to be there when a royal baby 93rd in line to the throne is born, rather than simply checking Twitter like the rest of us.

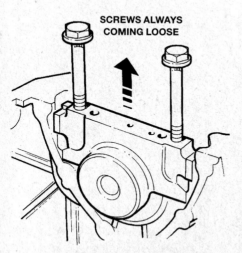

SCREWS ALWAYS
COMING LOOSE

FIG 10•3 **THE ANGLO-AMERICAN SPECTROMETER: HOW THE AMERICANS SEE THE BRITISH**

Of course, there are many things Americans find bewildering about the British.

a) Narrow streets and small cars. Not least because many of said streets are pre-America, let alone pre-cars.

b) Overcooked vegetables. 'How long's the broccoli been in?' 'About a week.' 'Oh, better give it half an hour more.'

c) Reserve. Americans will tell you their life story, including how much they earn and their sexual problems, within 12 minutes of meeting you. After a year of working with a Brit, he might volunteer that he felt a little down on one occasion.

d) Money. All American bills look the same, regardless of denomination. British notes look like the United Colours of Benetton. Sorry – the united colors. No 'u'.

e) That's another one. Spelling. Why the 'u' in 'colour' and 'favourite'? Why the 'e' in 'gray'? And what fresh hell is trying to pronounce 'Leicester', 'Bicester' and 'Featherstonehaugh'?

f) Tipping etiquette. Americans tip bar staff extravagantly, where the Brits might grudgingly say 'keep the change' or 'have one for yourself'.

g) Cricket.

How the Americans see the French

'France has neither winter nor summer nor morals. Apart from these drawbacks it is a fine country.' So said Mark Twain, and in the eyes of America little has really changed since then. The Americans don't quite know what to make of the French. In many ways they're rather similar countries: much of their system and many of their values can be traced back to their respective revolutions in the late 18th century, and they both believe that the world could do worse than adopt their culture and language.

But in many other ways they're different. Americans are puritanical, concerned with efficiency, and fiercely individualistic; the French are hedonistic, concerned with manners, and value the collective. So the American attitude towards the French remains mixed. On one hand, they see the French as the impossibly cool kid at school. They think France is beautiful (which it is) and that French food and wine knocks their American equivalents into a cocked hat (which they do). On the other, the Americans sneer at the French reluctance to get too involved with modern-day wars, are wary that the French flirt with socialism more than Americans could ever dream of doing, and most of all can't understand why the French don't speak English (like the Canadians and the British).

How the Americans see the Germans

When Americans think of 'German', they think of Teutonic precision. German cars – particularly Audi, BMW, Mercedes and Porsche – are a byword in the US for sophisticated reliability. For those who like their firearms (and there are apparently one or two such folk in the US), there's Heckler & Koch and Walther.

Some older Americans may still hark back to the war, but most of the middle-aged and younger generations neither know nor care too much about that. A German on holiday in the US is far more likely to be quizzed about (a) beer (b) what it feels like to drive at 180mph on an autobahn.

Americans see a lot of themselves in Germans, especially in terms of being hardworking and direct (though the German brand of directness is perhaps less overtly friendly than the American, unless of course you're in New York City, in which case Klaus is going to fit right the f**k in, you know?).

Rust prevention

Plastic surgery

When it comes to plastic surgery, Americans are right up there with any other nation. 'She's had work done' is not a sly insult, as it would be in other countries: it's a sincere appreciation both of the person in question wanting to maximise their appearance and of the surgeon who has (hopefully) done a good job. Except of course when that surgeon hasn't. The only thing that Americans appreciate more than a good plastic surgery job is a terrible one, because they can then thank their lucky stars that they couldn't afford the surgeon in question.

The comedienne Joan Rivers was very upfront about her (repeated) trips to the plastic surgeon. 'I saw what was going on under my chin. I didn't want to be the one the president had to pardon on Thanksgiving. I've had so much plastic surgery that when I die I'll donate my body to Tupperware.'

WARNING

If a friend asks you to lend them money for plastic surgery, think carefully. You won't know who to look for to get your money back.

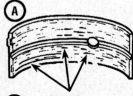
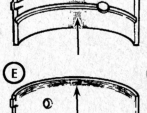

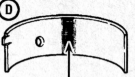

BRACHIOPLASTY
ARM LIFT, TO CORRECT SAGGING OF THE UPPER ARMS

OTOPLASTY
EAR SURGERY TO IMPROVE THE SHAPE, POSITION OR PROPORTION OF THE EAR

DYNASTY
SOAP OPERA STARRING JOAN COLLINS AND A BEWILDERING ARRAY OF SHOULDER PADS

FIG 10•4 **A SELECTION OF PLASTIC SURGERY TERMS AND THEIR MEANINGS**

⚠ US lawyers

The US has more lawyers than anywhere else in the world, both in absolute and per capita terms. Americans are obsessed with the law (the legal thriller writer John Grisham pointed out that the law was the one area of American life in which men and women were equally interested). The US spends more than $250bn on lawsuits every year, and two new suits are brought every second.

Most of these lawsuits are in general pretty sensible and bog standard. But some of them, er, aren't....

a) A man sued Anheuser-Busch for false and misleading advertising, claiming that, contrary to their slogan, beautiful women didn't actually come to life when he drank Bud Light. He added – when it comes to dumb lawsuits, in for a penny, in for a pound – claims for emotional distress and mental injury.

b) A woman sued Universal Studios on the grounds of extreme fear, mental anguish and emotional distress. She'd been visiting their Halloween Horror Nights haunted house and found it too scary. (Presumably if she hadn't found it scary she'd have sued for false advertising.)

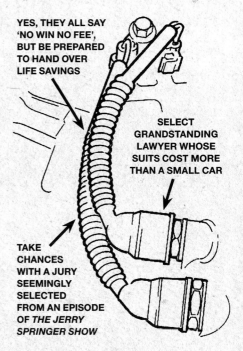

YES, THEY ALL SAY 'NO WIN NO FEE', BUT BE PREPARED TO HAND OVER LIFE SAVINGS

SELECT GRANDSTANDING LAWYER WHOSE SUITS COST MORE THAN A SMALL CAR

TAKE CHANCES WITH A JURY SEEMINGLY SELECTED FROM AN EPISODE OF *THE JERRY SPRINGER SHOW*

FIG 10•5 **THE LEGAL PROCESS: A HANDY GUIDE**

c) A man sued NBC on the grounds that an episode of *Fear Factor* in which the contestants ate rats caused him 'suffering, injury, and great pain' – specifically, made him dizzy, which caused him to vomit and run into a doorway.

These people all have two things in common. One, they're idiots. Two, the courts thought so too and threw the cases out.

Model behaviour

Conspiracy theories

The Americans do like a good conspiracy theory. Although any interaction which the average citizen has with the government almost always demonstrates that the government has enormous and perhaps terminal problems distinguishing between its arse (sorry – its ass) and its elbow, this doesn't deter millions of people from thinking that the selfsame government is a ruthless purveyor of insanely complicated conspiracies involving inside jobs, false flags, crisis actors and a ton of other stuff.

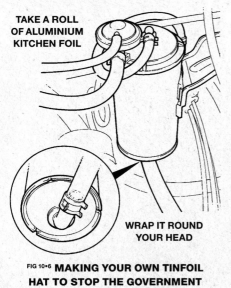

TAKE A ROLL OF ALUMINIUM KITCHEN FOIL

WRAP IT ROUND YOUR HEAD

FIG 10•6 **MAKING YOUR OWN TINFOIL HAT TO STOP THE GOVERNMENT READING YOUR MIND**

The Top Five conspiracy theories

1) One World Government/The Illuminati/The New World Order/ The Bilderberg Group. Basically, a secret group is controlling the world and trying to create a single government. If so, they're not doing a very good job of it given how many people seem to be fighting each other. Ah, they say, but that's the plan. It is? (This is also the conspiracy theorist's ultimate comeback: that any inconsistencies can be explained away as being part of the Master Plan which we're all just too stupid to see). An offshoot of this is the Lizard People theory, which holds that many powerful people are shapeshifting reptilian aliens. Sure they are.

2) Talking of aliens, there's the whole Area 51/Roswell conspiracy, which holds that an alien craft crashed in New Mexico and the occupants were taken to a top-secret military base called Area 51. (Not to be confused with Studio 54, which was a famous New York nightclub in the Seventies. One was a strange place full of bizarre creatures doing incomprehensible things. The other was Area 51.)

3) The moon landing was faked. Filmed in a studio, you know. Maybe by Stanley Kubrick. The name 'Neil A' spelt backwards makes 'alien'. How much more obvious do you want them to make it? Wake up, sheeple! (Like many conspiracy theories, it would actually have just been easier to go to the damn moon than it would have been to fake it.)

4) Chemtrails. You know those trails high in the sky? They're not from planes. No. Honestly. They're from chemicals sprayed by the government to control the population. Memo to chemtrailists: anything you see in the sky is (a) a jet's vapour trail (b) a cloud (c) a light aircraft trailing a banner saying 'You are a doo-doo head'.

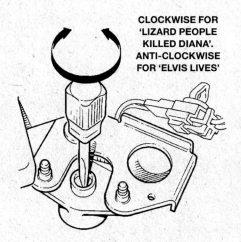

CLOCKWISE FOR 'LIZARD PEOPLE KILLED DIANA'. ANTI-CLOCKWISE FOR 'ELVIS LIVES'

FIG 10·7 **THE CONSPIRACY THEORY DIMMER SWITCH. THE DIMMER YOU ARE....**

There is of course the possibility that all these conspiracy theories are part of one overarching conspiracy. For example, Elvis killed JFK before hiding out with aliens in Roswell who helped fake the moon landings.

5) JFK assassination. Lee Harvey Oswald took the blame and Jack Ruby's bullets too – assassinating the alleged assassin means we can't assess from the alleged assassin's assertions whether or not he was the actual assassin. (Now try saying all that again when you've had a few.) But more than half of Americans believe either that Oswald didn't shoot JFK or that if he did then he didn't act alone. Prime suspects include the CIA, the mafia, the Soviets, the Cubans and the librarian to whom Kennedy gave the bum's rush when she tried to charge him $1.28 for the late return of *Gone With The Wind* back in 1949.

Service intervals

America is famous for its holidays – the Fourth of July, Thanksgiving, Labor Day, Martin Luther King Day, and so on. But there are also many days which aren't holidays but are given over to a variety of causes, no matter how obscure and niche. A quick flick through the calendar reveals the following chosen at random. Random being the operative word. May's entry, for example, will make people think you got dressed in the dark and/or are a little simple.

11 January
National Step In A Puddle And Splash Your Friends Day. Presumably you might not have too many friends left to splash if you do this too enthusiastically. Also perhaps not the best timing, given half the country is frozen solid in January.

19 February
National Lash Day. This is nothing to do with either S&M or going out on the piss. It's 'a day to promote the love and need for true and false eyelashes. Eyelashes are a true necessity for every person at any age.' What next? National Breathing Day? Nothing personal here, but this is surely the answer to a question which no one ever asked?

8 March
National Proofreading Day. 'This day promotes mistake-free writing and was created to bring awareness to the importance of proofreading.' Actually originally intended to be on April 8th, but no one caught the mistake before 200,000 flyers went to the printers.

6 April
National Sorry Charlie Day. Named after the StarKist cartoon mascot Charlie the Tuna, who was often rejected but always kept going. 'This day encourages us to think about the times we have been rejected.' Would therefore perhaps have been better round about Valentine's Day, just to REALLY rub it in.

3 May
National Two Different Coloured Shoes Day. 'Wear two different coloured shoes and see where they take you.'

21 June
National Selfie Day. Of all the things in the world, surely the last one which needs a special day is the selfie? Not sure if you've ever been on social media, Mr/Ms Originator of National Selfie Day, but every day is a selfie day nowadays. A national no-selfie day would be a much better idea.

24 July

National Thermal Engineer Day. Chosen because it's usually a hot day and is therefore perfect to celebrate the work of the thermal engineer.

8 August

National Sneak Some Zucchini Into Your Neighbor's Porch Day. Or, if you're English, National Give Your Neighbour A Courgette. There's so much that's weird about this. Who the heck 'sneaks' a zucchini in like it was a Valentine's card? Is that the best way you can think of to show your neighbour your appreciation?

8 September

National Ampersand Day. To celebrate the '&' sign. Suggestions for how to do this include substituting '&' for 'and' in words such as '&roid' and 'c&elabra', and sending missives to friends and relatives such as '&y', '&rea', 'Alex&er' and 'Gr&ma'.

9 October

National Kick Butt Day. Sadly, this is a metaphorical kick up your own butt ('Have you been meaning to start an exercise program or a diet? Are you wanting to change jobs? Do you have projects around the house you need to accomplish?') rather than an actual kick up the butts of random passers-by, which would be more (a) entertaining (b) likely to start a fight.

12 November

National Pizza With The Works Except Anchovies Day. Sorry, but this is anti-anchovy discrimination pure and simple. Olives, pepperoni, sausage, mozzarella, peppers, onions, mushrooms, gorgonzola, bacon and pineapple are all OK, but not anchovies? Someone call a lawyer.

25 December

A'Phabet Day or No 'L' Day. No 'L', as in 'Noel'. This may be the worst pun ever. Even Haynes Explains would think twice about putting this kind of pun down on paper. Especially when it goes on to say 'see if anyone catches on to the pun by avoiding the letter L in correspondence.' Correspondence? It's Christmas Day. Everyone will be either asleep in front of the TV or resurrecting centuries-old family feuds.

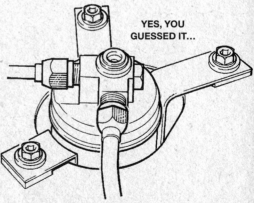

YES, YOU GUESSED IT...

FIG 10•8 **THERE'S A NATIONAL PLUG-IN DAY FOR OWNERS OF ELECTRIC CARS**

Fuel economy

As Fran Lebovitz said, Americans 'don't think time is money. They think everything is money.'

There's more than a whiff of truth to this. One of the most basic tenets of the American Dream is that anyone can be a millionaire, if they're prepared to put the work in. Someone driving a nice car in America will receive admiring glances, whereas someone driving a nice car in Britain will receive plenty of advice about where to go forth and multiply, the exact nature of their parentage and the suggestion that they are no strangers to onanism.

In many countries, a rich man or woman who seeks public office has to spend half their time downplaying their wealth or explaining how they came by it. Americans, in contrast, are very used to rich people running for high office. Both the current President and the previous Mayor of New York are billionaires, and plenty of other extremely wealthy people have fought and/or won elections. Given the cost of running political campaigns, the quickest way for a candidate to have a small fortune is to start with a large one.

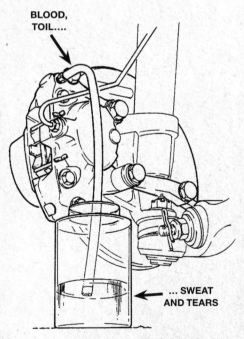

BLOOD, TOIL....

... SWEAT AND TEARS

FIG 10•9 **MILKING IT: MAKING A FORTUNE IN AMERICA**

Americans love to spend, even – or especially – when they can't really afford it. Unlike the Germans, who have a horror of credit cards, Americans will happily put it on the plastic and worry about it later.

⚠ American attitudes to retail

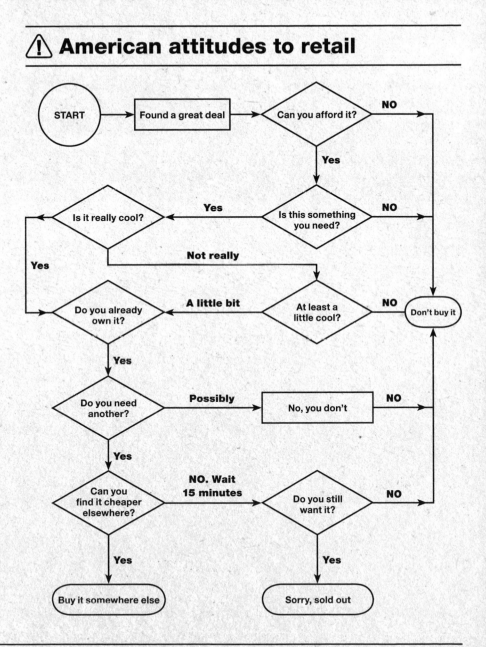

START → Found a great deal → Can you afford it? → **NO**

Can you afford it? → **Yes** → Is this something you need?

Is this something you need? → **NO** → Don't buy it

Is this something you need? → **Yes** → Is it really cool?

Is this something you need? → **Not really** → At least a little cool?

Is it really cool? → **Yes** → Do you already own it?

At least a little cool? → **A little bit** → Do you already own it?

At least a little cool? → **NO** → Don't buy it

Do you already own it? → **Yes** → Do you need another?

Do you need another? → **Possibly** → No, you don't

No, you don't → **NO** → Don't buy it

Do you need another? → **Yes** → Can you find it cheaper elsewhere?

Can you find it cheaper elsewhere? → **NO. Wait 15 minutes** → Do you still want it?

Do you still want it? → **NO** → Don't buy it

Can you find it cheaper elsewhere? → **Yes** → Buy it somewhere else

Do you still want it? → **Yes** → Sorry, sold out

⚠ Model variations

State	Handy shorthand (read: clichés)
Alabama	Rednecks. College football. NASCAR.
Alaska	Last refuge of the wild man explorer. Huskies and moose.
Arizona	The world's largest, and hottest, retirement home.
Arkansas	The kind of place where the family tree doesn't fork.
California	Surfers, beach bums, movie stars and tech billionaires.
Colorado	Stoners. Skiers.
Connecticut	Hedge fund paradise. More country clubs per square mile than anywhere else in the world.
Delaware	The first state to ratify the Declaration of Independence. Nowadays, the last state people remember. 'Here, we've got 49. Just can't think of the 50th.'
Florida	The world's second largest and second hottest retirement home (see Arizona). Also home to Disney, Crockett, Tubbs and the odd gator or 2 million.
Georgia	*Gone With The Wind*.
Hawaii	Surf. *Magnum, P.I.* Surf. Food. Surf. Hula. Surf. Volcanoes.
Idaho	Potato farmers.
Illinois	Chicago. Mafia. Corruption in City Hall.
Indiana	Tractors and the Indy 500.
Iowa	Cornfields as far as the eye can see.
Kansas	Tornado alley. Still seeking Dorothy and Toto.
Kentucky	Bluegrass, horses and fried chicken.
Louisiana	Voodoo, gumbo, jazz, Mardi Gras and Noo Awlins.
Maine	Don't like lobster? Sorry, pal, but your menu options are limited.
Maryland	Baltimore. The Wire. Preppy kids. (Not always mutually exclusive).
Massachusetts	Thank the Lord for spellcheck. The Bee Gees said they were going back there in 1967. No word on whether they've arrived.
Michigan	Shaped like a glove. Motor City.
Minnesota	Prince. Fargo. Snow. Scandinavians.

Mississippi	KKK. Blues music.
Missouri	Hunting. Two baseball caps: one for everyday and one for church.
Montana	Big sky. Small ranches are the size of Wales. Large ranches are the size of France.
Nebraska	'Hell, I even thought I was dead 'til I found out it was just that I was in Nebraska.' Gene Hackman, *Unforgiven*.
Nevada	Vegas. Elvis impersonators. Casinos. Showgirls. Shot a man in Reno.
New Hampshire	Holds the first primary in the US presidential election. Largely ignored for the other 207 weeks between elections.
New Jersey	You lookin' at me? You wanna piece, huh? How much do you bench?
New Mexico	Alien abduction and *Breaking Bad*. Crystal meth explains one and maybe both of these.
New York	So good they named it twice. Except the first time it was called New Amsterdam.
North Carolina	Barbecues and sweet tea.
North Dakota	Hacked off that South Dakota got Mount Rushmore.
Ohio	Swing state.
Oklahoma	State emblem: the deep-fat fryer.
Oregon	Hippies and Nike.
Pennsylvania	Blue-collar, steel and mines, *Rocky*, the Amish.
Rhode Island	Smallest state in the union. Not actually an island.
South Dakota	Mount Rushmore. Badlands National Park. Er… that's it.
South Carolina	Tobacco, moonshine and hillbillies.
Tennessee	Cowboy boots, whisky, country music.
Texas	Full of wide open spaces…. surrounded by teeth. Oil.
Utah	Where a man can cheat on his wife, but only with his five other wives.
Vermont	Maple syrup.
Virginia	Hunters, Civil War re-enactors.
Washington	Rain. Grunge. *Frasier*. Trees.
West Virginia	Strictly one tooth per resident.
Wisconsin	Cheese, cheese, cheese.
Wyoming	Where even the horses are Republican.

Language selection

There's an old adage which holds that Britain and America are two countries divided by a common language. Those defenders of the true English faith (and indeed the true English dictionary) may wish to stand by to repel the following.

a) 'Can I get a...?' As that annoying teacher at school would say: 'I'm sure you can, Smithers. The question is whether you may.' So too here. 'Please may I have?' is the correct form.

b) 'Gotten.' A slight on the perfectly serviceable 'got'. 'Gotten' is rotten.

c) 'Reach out.' As in 'has he reached out to you yet?' But all it means is 'contact', so just use the word 'phoned' or 'e-mailed'. If you're (a) a member of the Four Tops (b) stuck in quicksand (c) Adam and/ or God on the ceiling of the Sistine Chapel, then you can use the phrase 'reach out.' If you're not, then you can't.

d) 'Deplane.' For Heaven's sake. What's wrong with 'disembark'?

e) 'How are you?' 'I'm good.' Well, that's a matter of opinion.

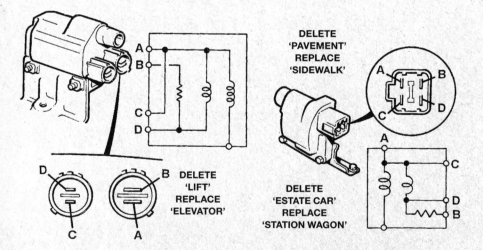

DELETE 'PAVEMENT' REPLACE 'SIDEWALK'

DELETE 'LIFT' REPLACE 'ELEVATOR'

DELETE 'ESTATE CAR' REPLACE 'STATION WAGON'

FIG 10•10 **NEURAL STRUCTURES SUBSERVING LANGUAGE PROCESSING**

f) 'My bad.' As in 'I have made a mistake.' 'My bad' is only acceptable when used in the literal sense, i.e. this is my copy of Michael Jackson's seventh studio album.

g) 'Oftentimes.' Why? How could you possibly either improve on or object to 'often'?

h) 'Going forward.' A meaningless management buzzword way of expressing a future strategy. 'What we're going to do, going forward, is….' When someone invents a time machine and people can go backwards in time, then and only then will 'going forward' be acceptable.

i) 'Regular Americano.' No, you corporate lickspittle. I just want a coffee. Or even a covfefe. I want a coffee to drink in my car, not a regular Americano to imbibe in my personal transportation device.

j) 'Where you at?' My fist is at a rapidly shortening distance from your nose if you insist on using this phrase.

k) Turning nouns into verbs. 'She medalled in three different events.' 'We're trialling this right now.' What next? 'Elizabeth II is queening real well at the moment'?

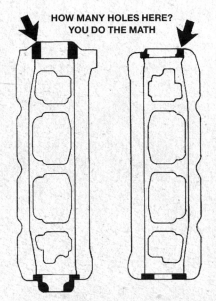

HOW MANY HOLES HERE? YOU DO THE MATH

FIG 10•11 **I REFUSE TO DO THE MATH. I WILL, HOWEVER, DO THE MATHS**

WARNING

These are not to be confused with the perfectly legitimate difference in meanings of given words. In Britain, the phrase 'I was so pissed that my pants ripped in two' means 'I was sufficiently drunk to have sustained substantial damage to my underwear.' In America, it means 'my trousers were inadequately made and as a result I am extremely angry.'

Road manners

By way of crass generalisation – our favourite sort at Haynes Explains – Europeans who drive in America may be shocked at how poor driving standards are. For many Americans, there is little incentive to be any more than an adequate driver. Roads are either deserted or choc-a-bloc. Cars are the size of houses and handle like bathtubs on wheels. Petrol is dirt cheap. Parking spaces and turning circles are sized to supertanker scale, though even this, plus every conceivable form of parking-assistance gadget known to man, still can't prevent most Americans from parking so far out in the road that they need a bus to get to the kerb.

Automatic cars

The vast majority of American cars have automatic transmissions, which means that for the vast majority of American drivers 'manual' is more likely to be the Mexican bloke they met last week than anything else. (Manual cars attract lower insurance premiums as they are deemed to be a theft deterrent. Seriously. Who knew car thieves were so picky? Actually, it's because many of those same car thieves literally don't know how to drive manual cars, which makes it even worse. No need for any of those steering-wheel locks, immobilisers and trackers. Just a gearstick will do the trick. In years to come, historians will surely date the start of the decline of the American empire from the moment one of Illinois' most promising young felons found a car with the keys in the ignition and the engine running, and instead of burning 50 feet of rubber just sat there trying to work the transmission out until the cops came to arrest him.

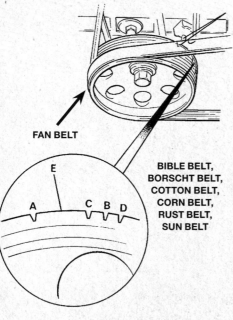

FAN BELT

E

A   C   B   D

**BIBLE BELT,
BORSCHT BELT,
COTTON BELT,
CORN BELT,
RUST BELT,
SUN BELT**

FIG 10•12 **AMERICAN BELTS – A GUIDE**

⚠ Americans and driving

Americans confess to doing all kinds of things behind the wheel (no, not THAT – which is to say they don't confess to that, not that they don't do it.) Three-fifths of Americans admit to reading the news or social media posts. Half ate a full meal (presumably without waiter service, though you can never be sure). A quarter popped a zit (if you're young enough still to be popping zits, surely you're too young to be driving? The Venn diagram on this one is surely not big on overlap). A fifth applied make-up, again presumably on the grounds that if you're going to crash then you might as well look good while doing so.

18% took a selfie. 8% vomited and 7% urinated. 3% shaved their legs. The question isn't just how these people got to the end of their journeys unscathed but surely how they passed their driving tests in the first place.

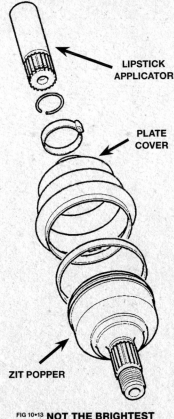

LIPSTICK
APPLICATOR

PLATE
COVER

ZIT POPPER

FIG 10•13 **NOT THE BRIGHTEST SPARK(PLUG)S OUT THERE**

WARNING

It is very inadvisable indeed to get involved with road rage incidents in America. In Britain, the worst you'll get unless you're very unlucky is a middle-fingered salute. In America, chances are that the driver with whom you're having a contretemps (a) has a gun (b) knows how to use it (c) is prepared to use it. And even if they don't, do you really want to take the risk?

Fuel

When you think of America, sooner or later (and let's be honest, it's usually sooner) you think of fat people. Certainly Americans themselves think like this too: the 'yo mama's so fat' meme is one of the most popular out there. You know the kind of thing. 'Yo Mama's so fat that she's got her own zip code.' 'Yo Mama's so fat that when she goes missing they put her picture on all four sides of the milk carton.' (A more British version would be 'your mother is so rotund that when she falls down the stairs

it sounds like the closing credits of Eastenders.)

In fact, Americans aren't the fattest nation on earth. Not even close. They're only tenth (and safe to say this is one world ranking they're happy not to be number one in). America can't even claim to be the fattest nation in North America (Mexico come in ninth) or the G20 (both Saudi Arabia and South Africa are higher, or rather wider). So the problem is one which is endemic to many parts of the world.

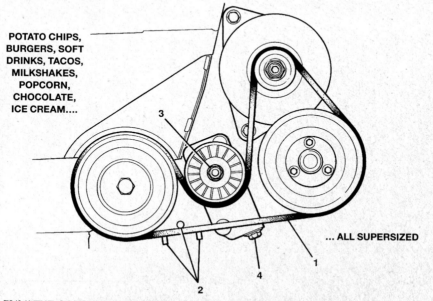

POTATO CHIPS, BURGERS, SOFT DRINKS, TACOS, MILKSHAKES, POPCORN, CHOCOLATE, ICE CREAM....

... ALL SUPERSIZED

FIG 10•14 **THE CONSUMPTION CONTRAPTION – AMERICA'S PERPETUAL EATING MACHINE**

⚠ Cookies

What makes all this even more extraordinary is that there are quite a few American foods which sound as though they have been deliberately designed to be very nearly or very actually inedible.

Biscuits and gravy, for a start. Which genius had that idea? It's not like any Briton has ever been rummaging around in the larder and gone: 'what have we got here? Some biscuits and some gravy. I know. I'll just mix the two together.' No, you fool! What fresh hell is this? Biscuits go with tea, roast chicken or beef goes with gravy. You're not some cutting-edge chef experimenting with molecular microfusion cuisine or whatever the newest fad is. You're just wrong.

And grits. Even the name 'grits' should give you a clue. Boiled corn ground into a coarse meal. Like porridge, but without the taste. Good for putting up wallpaper with. Bad for eating.

The Statue of Liberty has a 35-foot waist – or, as Americans like to call it, medium.

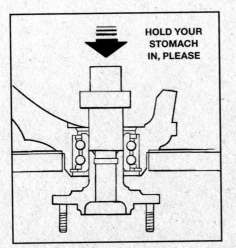

HOLD YOUR STOMACH IN, PLEASE

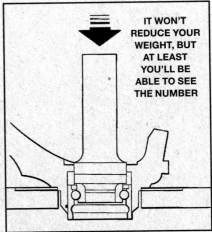

IT WON'T REDUCE YOUR WEIGHT, BUT AT LEAST YOU'LL BE ABLE TO SEE THE NUMBER

FIG 10•15 CALIBRATING YOUR BATHROOM SCALES THE AMERICAN WAY

Model history

1492

Christopher Columbus discovers America. The magnitude of this triumph is only slightly diminished by the fact that he thinks he's reached East Asia (he also thinks that Cuba is China and Hispaniola Japan.) On his return to Spain, his friends suggest a road trip on condition that Chris isn't let anywhere near map-reading.

SAILORS WHO'VE BEEN PROMISED TREASURE BUT INSTEAD HAVE TO SETTLE FOR A T-SHIRT SAYING...

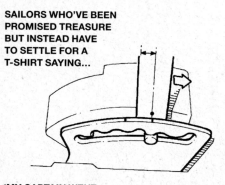

'MY CAPTAIN WENT TO NEW YORK AND ALL I GOT WAS THIS LOUSY T-SHIRT'

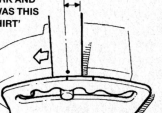

FIG 10•16 **THE FIRST ARRIVALS BY EUROPEAN EXPLORERS IN AMERICA**

1524

Giovanni di Verrazano discovers New York. He knows it's New York because the place is full of Italian-Americans standing with their arms folded saying 'I'm right here, alright?' and informing him that they ain't impressed, not even a little bit, with what he's done.

1692

Salem witch trials. Several young women are tried for witchcraft on the grounds that they've been screaming, throwing things, uttering peculiar sounds and contorting themselves into strange positions. It's three centuries until this behaviour is explained away not by anything supernatural but by rave music.

1732

Georgia becomes the 13th and last of the original colonies settled by the British. It's named after King George II, who scoffs at his courtiers' advice that 13 may prove an unlucky number. One American War of Independence later, his grandson George III admits there may have been something in that after all. He goes mad shortly afterwards.

1738

A young George Washington admits to chopping down his father's cherry tree with the words 'I cannot tell a lie.' He is the first and last politician to be able to say this with a straight face.

1773

The Boston Tea Party. Considering tea drinking to be British and therefore unpatriotic for good Americans, the locals chuck large consignments of British tea into Boston harbour. It is very much not the genteel tea party of cucumber sandwiches and 'more tea, vicar?' lore. In fact, if you substituted 'the groom' for 'consignments of tea' and 'Portsmouth' for 'Boston', you'd have a typical 21st century stag night.

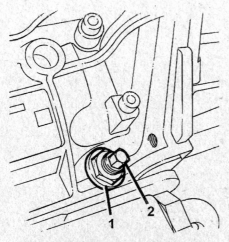

FIG 10•17 **APOLLO 11 NUTS. IMPORTANT TO MAKE SURE THEY'RE TIGHT**

1847

Brigham Young leads a group of Mormon pioneers westwards from Missouri. After 111 days, they come across the Great Salt Lake in Utah. Brigham orders them to stop and make permanent settlement because 'this is the place'. No one turns round and says 'Brig, old bean, it's 110 degrees, the water in that lake is undrinkable. This is very much not the f***ing place.'

1920-33

Prohibition. An idea so bad that to this day it is the only example of one amendment to the constitution (introducing prohibition) being repealed by another one (ending prohibition.) Responsible for, among other things, JFK's father making his first fortune and the ruining of a romantic 1929 Valentine's Day by a gangland massacre in Chicago.

1969

Neil Armstrong and Buzz Aldrin become the first men to walk on the moon. Armstrong says 'one small step for man, one giant leap for mankind'. Much to Sting's disappointment, Armstrong expresses no opinion on (a) whether or not his feet they hardly touch the ground (b) his feet don't hardly make no sound (c) the likelihood of his legs breaking while walking on, walking on the moon.

Recreational vehicle

Americans are very good at some of the sports which the rest of the world also play, such as track and field, swimming and golf. However, their three national sports are all disciplines at which America is (a) far and away the best in the world (b) the only people who play it (c) both.

Baseball

A grown-up version of rounders, basically. Played by men with horrible mutations whereby one hand has grown into an outsize leather mitt while the other remains normal.

Basketball

Come on. Basketball's all well and good as far as it goes, but it's impossible to take a sport seriously when a typical scoreline is 121-118, and even more impossible when the average player is 7'6" and has legs as skinny as pipecleaners. Besides, no matter how much you jazz it up with giant scoreboards, banks of seats and celebrity guests, a basketball court is always going to be only half a step away from being a municipal sports hall, with $3 for entry and don't forget some change for the lockers.

QUARTERBACK. 20-MILE
TAILBACK. NICKELBACK

WIDE RECEIVER. TELEPHONE
RECEIVER. WIDE BOY

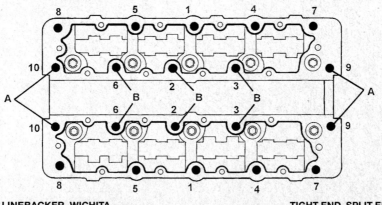

LINEBACKER. WICHITA
LINEMAN. OCEAN LINER

TIGHT END. SPLIT END.
HOWARD'S END

FIG 10•18 **AMERICAN FOOTBALL: A POSITIONING SCHEMATIC**

⚠ American Football

Not what the rest of the world term 'football'. No, that would be too easy. That's soccer. This kind of football is distinguished by being played with pretty much any part of the body other than the feet. Only 11 players can be on the pitch at any one time, which in football terms means a squad of 87,238 to cover offense, defense, special teams, extra laundry and traffic delays.

A typical passage of play:

1) The quarterback (usually blond, handsome and with impossibly white teeth) calls an insanely complex move such as '29 Mesh Lancaster Slide F-Shoot Y-Sail Moby'.

2) Everyone else nods enthusiastically without letting on that they have absolutely no idea what he's talking about.

3) A bunch of very large men on one side line up against a bunch of equally large men on the other side.

4) These men wrestle each other while the ball goes to the quarterback.

5) Anyone who's not wrestling with each other runs a zigzag pattern, or is it a crossfade, damned if I can remember, the hell with it, oh look, here comes the ball.

6) The quarterback's friend at wide receiver jumps high in the air to catch the pass. Upon landing, he is body-slammed by three of the opposition at once.

7) Play stops for 45 minutes while the quarterback assures the wide receiver that he is The Man and the wide receiver politely demurs on the grounds that surely the quarterback is in fact The Man.

Most professional American footballers are temperamental – they have a hell of a temper and they're totally mental. They also have amazing names, such as Plaxico Burress, Boomer Esiason, D'Brickashaw Ferguson, Barkevius Mingo and Lawyer Malloy (these are all real names).

In-car entertainment

What can sometimes seem like the vast majority of Western culture has originated from America. Hollywood is the world's most famous movie industry, even if its output nowadays seems to rely heavily on a range of improbably costumed superheroes battling against even more improbably costumed supervillains over who has the best CGI effects.

Before superhero movies were Westerns, which involved men who said one word every two hours and shot anyone who tried to strike up a conversation with them. And before Westerns were silent movies, which involved men who said no words every two hours and performed elaborate pranks on anyone who tried to strike up a conversation with them.

American television used to be seen as the poor relation of movies, but no more. American comedies are well known for having two dozen writers on every episode, each competing to shoehorn in as many of their own jokes as possible (or, failing that, to claim credit for Jeff's joke the moment Jeff goes off to the toilet – sorry, to the john. But John also goes to the john, not the jeff. It's very confusing). In addition, anyone who nails down the gig playing the brief twangy guitar riff during a scene change isn't going to go hungry anytime soon. A typical episode of *Seinfeld* involves at least 320 twangs.

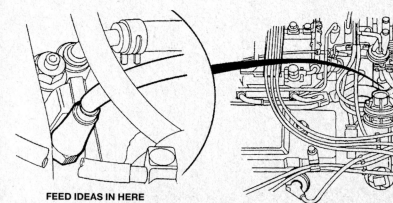

FEED IDEAS IN HERE

FIG 10•19 **THE SCREENWRITING PROCESS, AMERICAN STYLE**

American Music

Whatever your preferred musical genre, you can find it in America. If you woke up this morning to find your woman left you, there's the blues. If you have a mullet and can play three chords, there's rock. If you wish to make whiny pleas for sex, follow the signs to R 'n' B. And if you have a penchant for bling and don't think a ho is a garden implement, then you may well be a rap aficionado. Then there's the old favourite, country & western. What do you mean, they're separate styles? They are? Really? (googles frantically) Well, what do you know? Country music is simpler and uses fewer instruments, while western has a quasi-swing feel and tends towards steel guitars and big bands. And then there's bluegrass. Sorry, bluegrass. We haven't got room for you. You're just going to confuse the issue. On your bike.

Jackson Pollock was one of the leading American artists of the 20th century. He was most famous for drip painting. Jackson, dude, we were all doing that stuff in kindergarten.

Writers

For American writers, the holy grail is the Writing of the Great American Novel. Few of them ever manage it, if only because no one nowadays has the time or the patience to read 800 pages in which the worst thing that happens is that the Starbucks on 57th and Crenshaw temporarily runs out of soya milk. In contrast, writers of the past had great canvasses on which to pin their narratives – *To Kill a Mockingbird* (segregation and racism), *The Grapes of Wrath* (the Depression), *Gone With The Wind* (the Civil War), and so on.

SETTLING FOR THE GREAT AMERICAN TWEET

FIG 10•20 **CLAMPING ONTO THE ZEITGEIST**

⚠ An A-Z of Hollywood clichés

A
The standard of accommodation for the main characters is always ludicrously out of reach. A coffee shop barista making minimum wage will live in a loft-style apartment with views which a Fortune 500 CEO would be proud of. No wonder there was a subprime mortgage crash.

B
Binoculars are always represented by two circles in a Venn-diagram-style overlap rather than a single circle. The holder of the binoculars can never find what he's looking for first time: he must sweep across the scene, go too far and then double back when he realises he's nearly missed it.

C
Computer keyboards either beep or make exaggerated clickety-click noises while someone is typing on them. Everyone who uses them can touch-type to a speed unknown in the history of real-life office administration.

D
All government dossiers must be made from beige cardboard folders and feature an ancient passport photo of the character in question with a red stamp across the top saying 'LIQUIDATED' or similar.

E
Any engine which must be started urgently will turn over without catching while the bad guys close in and the protagonist shouts 'come on! COME ON!'.

F
During fight scenes, the bad guys who outnumber the hero eight to one will always obligingly attack him one by one rather than do the sensible thing and gang-tackle him.

G
No one ever says goodbye during a phone conversation.

H
Helicopters are the exclusive preserve of (a) villains (b) the FBI, who use them when they could just as easily walk.

I
Injuries never last for more than a few seconds and never disable a character for more than two scenes. In movieland there are no such things as concussion, whiplash or shock.

J
The hero will be able to jump absurd distances between rooftops when being chased and/or chasing someone. Anyone able to jump these distances in real life would make Olympic finals look like school sports day.

K
Keys are not necessary to open locked doors. Credit cards will do just as well.

L
The universal language is English (which is fair enough) and all foreign characters speak perfect though heavily accented English. The one word they consistently fail to master is 'yes', which they always say in their native language.

M

Monsters are always much more scary when you haven't seen them properly.

N

Anyone waking from a nightmare will sit bolt upright in bed with their eyes staring and their hair matted with sweat. They will then check the bedside digital clock.

O

Newly partnered cops will always begin as an odd couple who bicker and dislike each other. They will inevitably become bosom buddies before the closing credits are done.

P

Parking spaces are always available whenever any major character requires them. No movie has ever shown someone circling a multi-storey car park searching for the last available spot and prepared to cause a pile-up in order to secure it.

Q

Any character called Queenie – male or female, gay or straight – will be fearsome.

R

Bank robbers always bring holdalls which are exactly the right size for the haul they want to take with them.

S

After sex, all women sit up in bed with the sheet covering their breasts, and all men lie on their back with the sheet around their waist. You cannot buy sheets like this in the real world.

T

No taxi driver in the history of movies has ever been paid anything approximating the correct amount. He's either been tossed a bunch of bills and told to 'keep the change' or had the passenger leg it without paying. It all probably evens out in the end, come to think of it.

U

Protagonists can hold their breath underwater longer than most trained free divers.

V

Venetian blinds must only be used during scenes where a maverick cop is pleading for his job. While considering the issue, the boss may look out of the blinds before turning back and growling either 'you're off the case' or 'you got 24 hours'.

W

Whisky shots must always be drunk in one. Acceptable reactions following said consumption are (a) cough and splutter (b) go 'aaaaah' and smack lips (c) nod silently to the barman to indicate the need for a refill.

X

X-rays must always be left pinned against the lightboard for everyone to see. The hell with patient confidentiality.

Y

Any movie with the word 'you' in the title will be a romantic comedy so saccharine it will give you diabetes just by watching it.

Z

Any zone (e.g. factory, military) in an action movie will have to be cleared by whooping alarms and flashing lights sooner or later.

⚠ Fault diagnosis

Fault	Diagnosis	Treatment
Tendency to optimism.	American.	No treatment possible.
Believes self to be The Man.	American.	No treatment possible.
Likes sports the rest of the world don't play.	American.	No treatment possible.
Puts on weight just by looking at French fries.	American.	No treatment possible.
Owns more guns than shoes.	American.	No treatment possible.
Believes the government wants those guns.	American.	No treatment possible.
Drives cars which get 3 miles to the gallon.	American.	No treatment possible.
Listens to country and maybe western music too.	American.	No treatment possible.
Has a dozen lawyers on speed dial.	American.	No treatment possible.
Is more tribal about politics than about football.	American.	No treatment possible.
Thinks that every Englishman wears a bowler hat.	American.	No treatment possible.
Thinks that every Frenchman is a surrender monkey.	American.	No treatment possible.
Thinks that every German is nice but severe.	American.	No treatment possible.
Mangles the English language something rotten.	American.	No treatment possible.
Tells you their life story within half an hour.	American.	No treatment possible.
Can never have too many baseball caps.	American.	No treatment possible.
Believes the shopping mall to be heaven on earth.	American.	No treatment possible.
Sincerely admires someone who has made millions.	American.	No treatment possible.
Believes that anyone can be President.	American.	No treatment possible.
Flies the Stars and Stripes every day of the year.	American.	No treatment possible.

Conclusion

It's easy to take the rise out of Americans, especially in a book like this. It's easy because some of their national characteristics lend themselves to teasing, and also because it rectifies the balance of power in the tiniest of ways: they're the most powerful country in the world, and are liable to remain so for a while yet.

For most of its history America has been a force for good in the world. It has been the shining city on the hill of its own mythology. Heaven knows it's not perfect, but then again nor has been any country when it's been the most powerful on earth. American ideals of democracy, freedom and justice are the bedrock of Western liberalism.

And the Americans are in general an excellent bunch. Travel around America, and you'll find that 99 times out of 100 they're generous, warm and friendly. America is sometimes characterised as almost being two separate countries: the bicoastal areas east and west, where many of the large cities are and where most tourists go, and then the 'flyover states' in the middle.

From personal experience, if you fly over the flyover states then you're missing out. Utah, for example, is as staggeringly beautiful as anywhere on earth. The Deep South is full of heat and soul. There's even a certain mesmeric magnificence to the endless miles of farmland in the Midwest.

There are few countries which are so attuned to the joys of the roadtrip. In Britain a roadtrip involves three hours between cones on the M3 and running for cover from the rain whenever you have to stop. In America the horizon unspools before you. No one has ever crested an escarpment above Monument Valley and wished they were back in Kettering.

Just remember to go easy on the food, unless you want to pay for two seats on the return flight rather than one.

Titles in the Haynes Explains series

Now that Haynes has explained Americans, you can progress to our full size manuals on car maintenance (including all gas guzzlers), *BBQ Manual* (take on the US pros), *Boeing 747 Manual* (to get across the pond) and *U.S.S Enterprise Manual* (for all you Trekkies).

There are Haynes manuals on just about everything – but let us know if we've missed one.

Haynes.com